Mother Earth Rocks!
A Kid's Guide To Yellowstone National Park, USA

Photography By John D. Weigand
Poetry By Penelope Dyan

Bellissima Publishing, LLC
Jamul, California
www.bellissimapublishing.com

copyright © 2012 by Penny D. Weigand and John D. Weigand

All rights reserved. No part of this book may be
reproduced or transmitted in any form or by any means,
electronic or mechanical, including photocopying,
recording, or by any other means, or by any information or
storage retrieval system, without permission from the publisher.

ISBN 978-1-61477-062-6
First Edition

"*Our task must be to free ourselves... by widening our circle of compassion to embrace all living creatures and the whole of nature and it's beauty.*"

Albert Einstein

Mother Earth Rocks!
Bellissima Publishing, LLC

Introduction

Yellowstone National Park was duly established by the United States Congress and President Ulysses S. Grant on March 1, 1872. It is a national park located primarily in the U.S. state of Wyoming, although it also extends into Montana and Idaho. Yellowstone, the first national park in the world, is known for its wildlife and its many active geothermal features, especially the Old Faithful Geyser.

This book is a kid's look at Yellowstone National Park. And like award winning author, attorney and former teacher, Penelope Dyan, and photographer John D. Weigand, you may be surprised at what you see. The earth and the sky are alive, singing with the water and the trees and the land.

This is a different kind of kid's picture book, and like all of the Dyan/Weigand kids' travel books, they are meant to be carried in hand as adult counterparts carry their own travel guides. The verse is meant to teach learning concepts as it increases basic reading vocabulary skills through repetition and rhyme, Most of all, this book is meant to prepare the littlest of the travelers before they begin that big trip!

Mother Earth Rocks!
Bellissima Publishing, LLC

Mother Earth Rocks!
A Kid's Guide To Yellowstone National Park, USA

Photography By John D. Weigand
Poetry By Penelope Dyan

In Yellowstone National Park
there is a geyser called Old Faithful.
It is as reliable as it can be.
And everyone watches and waits
to see what they can see.
Then Old Faithful lets off steam
that rises toward the sky.
It almost always begins right on time,
and we can only wonder why.

As you watch, the steam plume grows.
It is very exciting, as everyone knows!
You think about our mother earth,
and about the miracle to which
it has here given birth.
How can this thing so wondrous be?
You wonder what else
on this trip you might see.

You see a bison,* an exciting site!
You wonder how you will sleep tonight.
There is excitement everywhere.
And a feeling of promise fills the air.

*The American bison is commonly rerferred to as the American buffalo.

Then of the bison you see even more, more than three, and more than four. You start to giggle, then you laugh, because they are right in front of you on the hiking path!

There is a winding river,*
and a lot more steam,
coming right out of the ground
right next to a stream!

*This is Midway Geyser Basin.

You see Geyser Cliff!
And it steams a lot!
(It looks just like a boiling pot!)
The earth seems FULL of miracles,
of water, earth, rocks and sand.
There are so MANY mysteries here,
all quite big, and all quite GRAND!

Then you see in the distance
coming out of the ground,
that even more steam escapes
from within a rock mound.*

*This is the White Dome Gyser.

And there is yet another place
where there is steam at its best!*
As to excitement,
Yellowstone has PASSED the test!

*This is Firehole Lake where the the Great Fountain Gyser can be found.

Mud paint pots bubble in Yellowstone
that really aren't paint.*
It comes right out of the ground,
and you think, "WOW! That's great!"

*This place is called "Artists Paint Pots."

And as you stand on a bridge's end
and you watch all that steam,
you wonder again,
"What CAN this ALL mean?"
Your mom exclaims, "The earth is alive!
It is a piece of creation
in which we ALL thrive!"
And you think about the clouds
and the blue of the sky,
and you feel that as to this place. . .
you should NEVER say goodbye.

And later, as you watch an elk rest
on a lawn of green,*
you wonder if this place
is simply a dream.

* You can find elk (if you are lucky) at Mammoth Hot Springs, near the Albright Visitor Center, part of a 1900 era cavalry post.

And although in your heart
you do long to stay,
you realize that from SOME things
you must just walk away!

"The poetry of the earth is never dead."

JOHN KEATS

www.ingramcontent.com/pod-product-compliance
Ingram Content Group UK Ltd.
Pitfield, Milton Keynes, MK11 3LW, UK
UKHW060134240426
12048UKWH00002B/29